Beyond Authorship:
Things Writers Should Know Besides How to Write

By Ed Mickolus

WANDERING WOODS PUBLISHERS

Beyond Authorship:
Things Writers Should Know Besides How to Write

By Edward Mickolus, PhD

ISBN: 978-1-949173-23-9

Published in the United States by
Wandering Woods Publishers
EdwardMickolus.com

Book Design, Cover and Typesetting by
Cynthia J. Kwitchoff (CJKCREATIVE.COM)

TABLE OF CONTENTS

Introduction

Writing a book isn't just about writing. You already know how to do that. At best, the actual writing is only half of the work that you'll put in to your book.

This book grew out of a series of 11 articles I wrote for a Florida Mensa chapter that were reprinted by the St. Louis-based Writers and Publishers Network. I added a few talking points used in courses I gave at the University of North Florida and presentations to various writers groups and Florida Writers Association chapters.

In it we'll examine issues that you should consider before starting to write, during the writing phase, and after publishing a book. We'll cover reasons for writing, enhancing your creativity, keeping up in your field and those of others, how to be prolific, collaborating with a colleague and multiple colleagues, the care and feeding of character bibles to ensure continuity, the two main types of publishing, dealing with marketing, and polishing your skills as a presenter. Alas, none of this is the fun part—writing—but is absolutely essential to your success if you want to go beyond writing for just yourself.

There are lots of books that cover marketing, social media, and financial issues, so I'll protect your time and won't plow the same ground.

Why Write?

So enough about me. Let's talk about you.

Why are you considering writing? As the designated Smartest Person in the Room, how many times have friends/colleagues/enemies said to you, "You know, you should write a (book/screenplay/short story/tweet)" or something similar? Or after reading a piece of prose, you've thought "Jeez, I could do better than that!"

Has this been enough to get you to writing? Probably not, and it shouldn't.

Writing—at least for enjoyment—is something that you want to do, not something suggested by invidious comparison, or imposed by the outside (unless you're doing it as part of your job, in which case, it's work, not necessarily fun).

So back to square one: What inside you is saying "I want to write"? I asked members of several writers groups in which I participate; their answers tend to cluster around:

- ❑ I'm motivated to write to give of myself, my thoughts, hopes, dreams, solutions.

- ❑ I'm curious to see if I have it in me.

- ❑ I have interesting stories to tell.

❑ I enjoy self-expression via the written word. (It's ok if you're also a talker. Sometimes spoken and written media can feed off each other.)

❑ I have a message I want to convey to others.

❑ I want to make money. (Be careful in your expectations. A tiny percentage of the self-published books in America sell even one copy! Don't expect to rival Grisham and Patterson. However, at the other end of the spectrum, a friend's letter to a store "complaining about a product was so well written that they have kept it and often give me quiet discounts. Possibly they're worried I will complain nationally but they did ask me if I was a writer!" So she's a successful writer, and is perceived as a writer. What else can you ask for!?)

❑ I want my memoirs to be my legacy to my family and/or The Next Generation.

In my case, I write my terrorism and intelligence nonfiction

■ to still be useful to those battling evil. I had a 33-year career at the Agency and taught young intelligence officers for another five years. Although I've handed off the baton to a new generation (by now, several generations—jeez, I'm getting old!), I can still help.

■ to make an impact

■ to leave a legacy

Making money is way down on my list. So I'm not frustrated when I tell you that I'm famous among 400 people and never quit my day job.

Where Do You Get Your Ideas?

Authors working in any genre are inevitably faced with the dreaded question, "Where Do You Get Your Ideas?" In many cases, "I don't know, they just come to me," may be true, but unsatisfying to your interlocutor, who may view you as coy because they were hoping that you'd share some trade secret that will make them part of the writing inner circle.

This openness to ideas coming from the blue is consonant with the "pantser" type of writer, who follows characters wherever they take him/her, working without an outline, or without a net.

Adherents of the "outliner" writing tribe will flock to a more rigorous approach to creativity.

Creativity can be seen as having specific phases:

- Setting the right environment

- Clearing out mindsets and hidden assumptions that block new ideas

- Generating ideas

- Capturing Ideas

A separate endeavor regarding new ideas is Innovation—taking creative ideas to market. Its phases can include

- Selecting the best idea, using various criteria (cost, morality, efficiency, time constraints, acceptability to others)

- Prototyping (try it, be willing to fail on a small scale, learn from the experience. If you're not failing, you're not stretching yourself. Edison tried some 9,000 filaments before he got the light bulb correct. He just viewed them as setting aside 9,000 things he no longer needed to pursue.)

- Implementing/rollout (write it, publish it)

- Evaluating (Did the book sell? What did the reviews say? Did you enjoy the process?)

While most of these concepts are more readily relevant to product development, we can look at our writing as the to-be-finished product and apply the same principles.

Setting the environment entails asking yourself: Where am I the most creative? Where do I get most of my new ideas? Is it staring at a computer screen, stressing yourself out over a self-imposed deadline?

For some, yes. For others, it's getting away from intellectual pressure, and doing something that lets left brain take a rest and gives right brain a chance to come out and play.

Many colleagues tell me new ideas intrude while driving, running, walking in the park, swimming, playing a physical game (e.g., tennis, pickleball, bowling, bocce) or showering. (Writers are a proud people, and a clean people!) I get mine polishing silver.

All of these endeavors set aside left brain's logical, rule-based, step-by-step attentiveness. Simple tasks involving muscle memory allow the brain to pay attention to other things, with new ideas sprouting.

Others find new ideas in dreams, to the extent that they can remember them. Always have a pen and paper on your nightstand so that you can capture those wacky ideas during the night.

Buy my books, or the people
who use "its" instead of "it's" win.

NOTES:

Creativity Tips and Techniques

In the last chapter, we started examining the phases of creativity. Let's take a look at what can get in your way, and what can help, in generating and capturing new ideas.

One should be attentive to one's **biases, mindsets**, and unstated/hidden/culturally-bidden **assumptions**. Conventional thinking gives us useful patterns to predict what will happen in a given situation. If we believed we were facing absolutely new situations every second, we'd cower in fear. Pattern-seeking gives us a sense that the world is orderly and we can operate within it. Such norms can derive from myths, lore, and success. But when the environment changes, over-reliance on conventional wisdom can be our downfall.

Those pesky hidden assumptions are difficult to spot, because they feel like they're Revealed Truth, hard-wired to our brains. For example, why is a keyboard organized as QWERTY? Because in the dawn of ergonomic thinking, typewriter designers wanted to slow down proficient typists, who outsped the capability of the keys to get out of the way of the next keystroke, causing traffic jams.

While many believe that QWERTY was designed to be the most efficient keyboard layout, it is actually one of the least efficient. But for us to change to a new keyboard would require a massive change to our muscle memory.

A common assumption is that there is only one right answer, which comes from our early arithmetic training. 2 + 2 = 4 (except for very large values of 2!). But what if we reframe the question, and not make it a math problem? Are there other right answers? 2 + 2 is an automobile layout. 2 + 2 is a song lyric. Consider whether you're asking the right question. Try reframing it. Einstein suggested that the preponderance of your time should be spent on figuring out what question to ask, and only after that should research proceed.

While creativity in **idea generation** has a rich literature, it all comes down to two simple concepts: change in perspective and associations.

In **perspective creativity**, one merely looks at an issue from a different angle. Are we correctly framing the question? What if we changed one aspect of the issue? For example, what's half of 8? If we treat it as a math problem, half of 8 is 4. But what if we change our assumptions, and it's no longer a math problem, but a visual problem? Then half of 8 could be 0, 3, E, S, or 5. What if 8 weren't written in Arabic numerals, but in Roman? Then it could be VI or II. Or what if it's a spelling problem? It could be ei, or ght. Or what if it isn't spelled "eight" but "ate"? Or misspelled? Or in another language? Or in another base (not just decimal, but octal, hexadecimal, and all of their friends.). (Be sure you don't help your child with their math homework when doing this exercise. Their teacher won't buy it.)

In **associative creativity**, we try to meld two dissimilar ideas, often from different experiences/professions/cultures, and see what pops up at their verge. Hollywood screen playwrights use this technique all the time. Merge hot cheerleaders with scary ghouls and you get *Buffy the Vampire Slayer*. Merge spas and sci fi and you get *Hot Tub Time Machine*.

Fear of flying and fear of snakes yields *Snakes on a Plane*. Experimental chefs open fusion restaurants. Alternative fuel cars change assumptions about the centrality of combustion engines to the industry.

**Buy my books, or the weeds
will win control of your garden.**

NOTES:

Read Widely

We'll finish up our look at creativity with a few tips and techniques on making these approaches work for you.

One simple way you can incorporate associative creativity into your daily writing routine is to read widely outside your field. Read about art, architecture, astronomy, astrophysics (and that's just some of the As), looking for how they developed solutions.

Similarly, talk to people not steeped in the conventional wisdom of your specialty, who don't know "that's never worked", who don't have your unstated assumptions. Listen to your hairdresser, tennis partner, trivia teammates, your friends, accountant, plumber, electrician, about how they went about solving problems. How structurally, not substantively, similar were their quandaries to what you're currently facing? Can you adapt their strategies to your situation?

One simple way of getting new ideas: **Ask What If?** What if your character changed this aspect of her/his life? What if the environment in which they operate changed? What if they lost their job, their home, their marriage, got shot, won the lottery, was First Contact with an alien, discovered something unexpected in their background?

In nonfiction, what if conventional thinking about an issue is wrong? What are the contending hypotheses? What if we're measuring the wrong variables? What if we're not measuring what we think we are?

In this phase, by the way, just let the ideas flow. Don't self-edit. Write them all down, no matter how goofy. Editing is in a downstream phase—what we called "selecting the best idea" in our litany of Innovation phases.

Idea capture is crucial. Whatever the source of your new ideas, be prepared for synchronicity to strike at the most inconvenient time, and write down the idea before it's lost. Many of the great inventors credit their success solely to having the presence of mind to write down their insight asap.

Whatever your style of creativity, be ready for that new idea—it's opportunity knocking, and if you don't answer, it might go to the next door.

Buy my books, or Skynet wins.

Read Widely, But Also in Your Field

We've examined earlier the importance of getting input from sources outside your area of expertise. Different perspectives on problem-solving can assist you in looking at an issue differently, and adapting those insights into your solutions.

It's also important to keep up with the literature in your specialty, for different reasons.

- You can provide useful prepublication feedback to the author. It's preferable if you get a copy of the book in beta form, or at least in its blurb phase, before it's published, so that you might protect the author from the occasional typo and/or factual misstatement. When I was an editor, I'd routinely share a publication with up to 14 different proofreaders. No matter how finicky you are as an editor—and I suspect that "finicky" will appear somewhere on my tombstone—you're going to miss things and be happy that someone had your back during proofreading/fact checking.

- If you're not that close to the author or publishing house, you can at least contact the author after the book's release to make suggestions for tweaking the second printing of the book.

- By the way, it is far preferable to contact the author quietly, rather than write a scathing review. You'll make enough enemies in your writing career; you don't need to manufacture any others. Contacting the author privately increases the likelihood that you can help improve the book; trashing it in a review makes it likely that they'll toss your comments aside.

- You'll learn a factoid or two.

- You'll see how fellow experts have a different twist on the same data you're analyzing.

- When you're being interviewed on a podcast, tv, or radio show or serving as a panelist at an academic or professional conference, you don't want to be blindsided by someone referring to a major article/book that has attracted widespread notice.

- You may discover that you're so in sync with the thoughts of the author that you'd like to approach them to co-author a study.

For example, I recently finished reading Dennis A. Pluchinsky *Anti-American Terrorism: From Eisenhower to Trump—A Chronicle of the Threat and Response, Volume II: The Reagan and George H. W. Bush Administrations* Singapore: World Scientific, 2020, the sequel to his earlier look at U.S. terrorism policy in previous administrations. He's now merrily writing Volumes III and IV.

Dennis analyzed terrorism trends for the U.S. Department of State for decades; we started our careers together. There's no one better positioned to speak authoritatively about the evolution of U.S. anti-terrorism policy than Dennis. Drawing upon my just-released *Spycraft for Thriller Writ-*

ers, I've shared with him a few observations on intra-CIA terminology, as well as the genesis of my International Terrorism: Attributes of Terrorist Events databases he cites with approval, for his upcoming volumes. I'm looking forward to the opportunity to beta (and it that's not a word, it should be!) Volumes III and IV.

***And remember: buy my books,
or the terrorists win!***

NOTES:

Be(com)ing a Prolific Author

Some of us write just one book and call it a career. Others call that a promising start.

Some prolific writers became famous:

- **Sophocles** reportedly wrote 123 plays, although only seven survived, so how can we be sure he hit that number?

- **Shakespeare** was good for 38 plays and 154 sonnets.

- **Georges Simenon** wrote 500 novels, 200 in true name, 300 in a dozen pseudos. Some of his books introduced us to French literature.

- **R.L. Stine** is in the hundreds.

Your name doesn't have to begin in S:

- **Alexandre Dumas** is credited with 277 books, although he told Napoleon III that he'd written 1200 titles, many of them collaborations

- **Jozef Ignacy Kraszewski**, aka **Kleofas Fakund Pasternak**, logged 600 books

More famous authors from the 20th century:

- Our favorite Mensa member, **Isaac Asimov**, while teaching biochemistry at Boston University, wrote 506 books (and covered nine of the ten Dewey decimal categories!).

- **Enid Blyton** wrote 800+ books for children, sold 600 million copies, and was translated into 90 languages

- **Ben Bova** wrote 120 novels.

- **William F. Buckley, Jr.,** edited *National Review,* hosted *Firing Line,* ran for NYC Mayor, and wrote 58 books, including 34 nonfiction, 4 travel, and 20 novels. His son Chris has so far written 20 books.

- **James Earl Carter** wrote 32 books, and, oh yeah, served as U.S. President

- Romance novelist **Barbara Cartland** wrote 722 novels, including 23 in one year.

- **John Crease**y wrote 600+ novels, using 28 pseudonyms, including Margaret Cooke when he wrote romance. He was rejected 768 times before his first publication was accepted. Take heart!

- **Charles Hamilton** wrote 100 million words under 20 pseudonyms, equivalent to 1,200 novels

- **Stan Lee** wrote one comic book per day for ten years.

- **Francine Pascal** had written 181 *Sweet Valley High* novels as of May 2020.

- Romance novelist **Nora Roberts** has written 225 novels, and counting.

- **Rabindranath Tagore** penned 2,232 songs and 50+ volumes of poetry

- **Sir Pelham Grenville Wodehouse** wrote 96 novels, 40 plays, and 200+ short stories

Several contemporary authors are putting up big numbers:

- **David Baldacci** has written 63 novels, including seven for young adults, selling 150 million copies in 80 countries. They have been translated into 45 languages.

- **Harlan Coben** has written 37 novels since 1990, some 80 million are in print in 40 languages. He has a deal with Netflix to make 14 novels into movies or tv series.

- **Michael Connelly** has written 40 books, selling 74 million copies in 40 languages. He also has time to executive produce the *Bosch* and *Lincoln Lawyer* tv series.

- **Jeffery Deaver** has written 51 titles, available in 25 languages in 150 countries. His books have been made into movies and the tv series *Tracker*.

- **John Grisham** has written 37 #1 best-sellers, and has had 47 titles on the *New York Times* best seller list. He has sold more than 300 million copies.

- **Steven King** has written 74 novels and 200 short stories and still has had time to play rhythm guitar for the Rock Bottom Remainders.

- **Dean Koontz** has written 105 standalone novels, 74 short stories, and three graphic novels, which have sold 450 million copies. His pseudonyms include David Axton, Deanna Dwyer, K.R. Dwyer, Leigh Nichols, and Brian Coffey.

- **Jean Marzollo** wrote 150 books, including the *I Spy* series.

- **Walter Mosley** has written 62 novels and 2 plays, which have been translated into 21 languages.

- **Joyce Carol Oates** has written 58 novels plus several plays, novellas, and short stories.

- **James Patterson** has written 200+ novels since 1976, selling 425 million copies. He is the first person to sell 1 million e-books.

- **Jodi Picoult's** 28 novels have sold 40 million copies in 34 languages.

- **Lisa Scottoline** has written 35 novels since 1993.

- **Will Shortz** wrote or edited 500+ puzzle books.

- **Joel Whitburn** wrote 200+ books, based upon his collection of more than 200,000 records, among them every single ever to make a Billboard chart.

Others aren't such household words:

- **Ursula Bloom** wrote 500 books, her first at age 7. She wrote so many that she needed numerous pen names, including Sheila Burns, Mary Essex, Rachel Harvey, Deborah Mann, Lozania Prole, and Sara Sloane.

- **Yoshitaka Fujii** was a Japanese anesthesiologist who allegedly fabricated his findings in at least 183 papers, according to a 2012 investigation launched by journal editors and Japanese universities.

- **Howard Garis** of the Stratemeyer Syndicate is credited with 500 young adult (YA) novels. Ed Stratemeyer developed plots for Tom Swift, the Hardy Boys, and pretty much anything that was published for juveniles from 1908 to about 1930, then gave it to "hack factories".

- Brazilian surgeon **Ryoki Inoue** wrote nearly 1,000 novels in six years under 39 pseudonyms. He's up to 1,075 books, the Guinness record.

- German author **Rolf Kulmuczak** wrote 2,900 novels under 100 pseudonyms.

- **Kathleen Mary Lindsay** wrote 904 books under 11 pseudonyms: Mary Faulkner, Margaret Cameron, Mary Richmond, Molly Waring, Betty Manvers, Elizabeth Fenton, Nigel Mackenzie, and Hugh Desmond.

- **Jacob Neusner** wrote or edited 950 books, most around 400 pages.

- **Ryohu Okawa**, head of the Japanese Happy Science religion, has published more than 2,000 titles, many of them transcriptions of his sermons.

- **Irna Phillips**, Queen of the Soaps, wrote two million words/year, often writing six daily radio and tv soap operas at once, including *The Guiding Light, As the World Turns, The Edge of Night*, and *Another World*, equivalent to 40 novels/year.

- **Corin Tellado** sold the most books written in Spanish, published more than 5,000 titles, and sold more than 400 million books.

- **Matt Zurbo** wrote 365 children's books in 365 days, while working full-time at an oyster farm.

A few of my friends in the Jacksonville, Florida area have also made the Prolific List, including Lana McAra, president of the local Sisters in Crime chapter and founder of Vendela Publishing, who has written 46 books, ghosting 20, which have sold one million copies. Dorothy K. Fletcher has written four books and seen her poems published in 78 literary journals (I'm impressed that her Rolodex includes that many journals!).

Others whose names are even lesser-known to us have generated thousands of books, of varying quality and length. There's probably a reason or two why you haven't heard of them, and none of these reasons are your fault.

What's their **secret(s)**?

Frankly, I don't know, but I can share with you techniques that I've used to write 60 books, 40 book chapters, and hundreds of articles for scholarly journals and newspapers. While I'll limit this discussion to books, I use the same techniques for articles in scholarly journals, teaching courses, newsletter profiles and fun articles, newspaper pieces, writing contests, Internet commentaries, and presentations at learned societies and civic associations.

Let's get back to you again. Write down:

- **What** you write or want to write—books, articles, etc.

- **Why** you write (see if you still have your notes from two months ago.)

- **Why** you want to be **prolific**

- **What prolific writing means to you**, either in sheer numbers, or some other measure. What level of output would satisfy you?

How you go about being prolific depends upon your answers to these questions.

I derive the **call to be prolific**

- Matthew 25: 14-30 instructs us to **use one's talents**. I might not be the best writer in the room, but I'm usually the fastest! I'm aware of what I'm marginally good at, and don't kill myself trying to do what I'm not good at. Remember comparative advantage in Economics 101? Do that, particularly if you enjoy it.

- As I age, I'm more aware of **looming mortality**, and I have a lot to get done before potential age-related ailments and eventual death halt my productivity.

Whatever your writerly motivations, much of the key to getting a lot done boils down to **time management** techniques.

The first thing to do is get organized. Set up your writing lair so that you can find things efficiently because they're where they should be.

Second, set goals—near term/tactical, short term, and long term. Write them down and keep that list where you will see it every day. You might believe that you have them in your head, but it's still useful for these lists to hit your eyeballs every so often as a reminder of what you're aiming for. Here are my writing projects (and if you know of any publishing houses that might be interested…):

Near Term: This year and next

- *Terrorism Worldwide 2025*

- *Beyond Authorship*

- *All the Presidents' Heroes: Inspirational Stories of State of the Union Honorees*, 7 volumes, for each President since Reagan

- *Famous Last Meals*

- *Stories by the Side of the Road*

Medium term—next year and the following year

- *Terrorism Worldwide 2026* and the sequels in the series

- *Naked Came the Spy*

- *Moscow Syndrome*

- *…And Presumed Dead*

Long term—3-10 years down the road

- *Kursk*—terrorists try to take over a Russian nuclear sub

- *Al-Seriali*—terrorists use serial killers as a tactic

- *Prez/Ex-Prez*—a down-at-the-heels country auctions off its presidency. The book follows the winner and his predecessor.

- *Collector*—a terrorist leader uses famous weapons

- *Narco*—a terrorist group poisons narcotraffickers' product

- *Predictor*—a terrorist uses sayings of Nostradamus as a guidebook for mayhem

- *First Tour*—an anthology of spy-fi short stories, using the same characters, tracking them through their careers. Follow-up volumes will include *Base Chief, Chief of Station, Division Chief, Director*

- *Murder in the Villages*, and a sequel: *Do Serial Killers Ever Retire?*

- *Defending Terrorists: The Lawyers*

- *Victims of Terrorism*

You'll note that I have **several projects going at once**, at **different stages of development**. This is a technique suggested by **Richard Armour**, a humorist from the 1950s and 1960s—the Dave Barry of his generation. He counseled lining up writing projects like **airplanes on a runway**, ready to take off, but at various stages of readiness in that queue.

Having multiple projects going simultaneously keeps your **writing and creative juices flowing, helping you avoid boredom, burnout, and writers' blocks**. Whenever one of those **killer B's** hits you on one project, just turn to the next—**Plan B**!

The technique has allowed me to be **engaged**, and to respond in real-time to **fast-breaking issues** in the world. When you're writing on intelligence, national security, international terrorism, politics, and propaganda, being a few hours out of date relegates you to the dustbin of history. If you're trying to make a difference, you have to make the difference now. You have to choose whether you're involved in making history, or merely writing about it later.

This method works for me for **non-fiction**. I recently listened to a prolific local author—she generates a book every six weeks—who writes **fiction seriatim, not consecutively**. Her reasoning is that you don't have to "reload" your brain every time you return to the book. You can remember continuity issues better if you're working on the same thing and let it consume your time.

She also argues that if you're strictly in it for the **money**, just focus on that goal. **Put out product**, and product in areas in which people are buying. Romance, erotica, mystery, thrillers sell. Literary masterpieces do not. Historical fiction is tough to write quickly. Make it easy to read. Make it **65-85K words**. Use **dialog and white space**. Do the intellectual heavy lifting for your audience—don't make them struggle to follow you. Don't use $5 words when dime-a-dozen words will do. Write book **series**—if they liked your character in this novel, they'll want to find out what happens next to him/her. Write in the form of **e-books**.

In addition to these long-term goals, have short-term, including **daily**, ones. I average about 800 words/day. By the end of the year, I've generated about 300K words. For a novelist, that's around five short novels. For my longer nonfiction books, that's a long book per year, plus a few articles.

Hitting these goals takes time, and you have to **balance** getting to those goals with what you're willing to not do to get to them.

You don't have to **sacrifice** everything, however. You can use time management and tracking techniques, such as my **spreadsheet**, which we'll examine a little later.

Just thinking about writing books, novellas, or long articles can be intimidating. How am I ever going to crank out 300 pages (or more)? The good news is that you don't have to do it all at once. As with any task in life, you can break up the most ambitious writing project into more digestible bits, then have at them in turn.

This PERT technique resonates well with "outliners" (a term often used for novelists who painstakingly plot out their "character bible" and plan their story line for months, then breeze through the actual writing), but also works for "pantsers" (novelists who don't outline, but let the strong characters lead them, seat-of-the-pants, until the plot finishes itself). Non-fiction writers tend to be planners on this continuum.

Pull out a grid, an Excel spreadsheet, or just a blank sheet of paper. On the top line (or X axis), write the names of all of the book/article projects you have in mind. On the side (Y axis), write all of the individual tasks needed to complete the project. You can be as specific as necessary—the more specific, the less intimidating each entry will be. This helps you track where you are in each of a book's phases.

Here's what works for the Y-axis for my non-fiction. Novels are slightly different, but not by much. Note that this is specifically designed for those who write for **conventional publishing**. You're welcome to try **self-publishing**, which we'll discuss in an upcoming chapter, and which will have slightly different phases.

- researching

- in outline (pantsers vs. planners)

- in first chapter

- in proposal form for agent and/or acquisition editors

- in completed first draft

- checking copyright of any photos, graphics, other artwork

- sharing proposed contract with your contract attorney (Do not accept "this is our standard contract, we don't make changes." It may well be their policy, but the agreement is between you and the publishing house, and you really should not care what the other authors signed.)

- for sharing with your colleagues/beta readers

- with strategic editors

- with acquisitions editors

- with copyeditors

- in galleys

- for sale (but requiring your marketing skills)

As you complete a task, you can either just put a checkmark into the appropriate square, or put a date on which you completed the task.

Breaking the project into **smaller bites**—saying "I'm doing Task 3C today"—is nowhere near as daunting as saying "I'm trying to write a 900-page book", a sentence that should be used only in cocktail parties and tenure meetings.

Next month we'll look at the steps needed to write a novel.

A few other habits I've found useful in writing:

- Always have **notepads** (or some other method of recording new but fleeting ideas) wherever you are—driving, dining, walking/running, showering, you name it. We lose ideas due to what Duke

University's Department of Psychology calls the Velcro Theory of Memory. New ideas don't have a batch of associations already built up in memory—there aren't enough "hooks" for the new idea to latch onto, so if we don't use some other method of retaining the memory—writing it down—it gets lost.

- [ ] **File** away those great ideas. You might not use them for the book you're currently writing, but they might be helpful for another project later on. Many prominent hardboiled detective fiction writers kept files of ideas on, say, murder techniques, hats, knives, settings, etc. for just such purposes.

- [ ] **Say yes to opportunity**; it won't keep knocking

- [ ] **See opportunities and adapt/repurpose.** Consider **MIRVing** (a term derived from the Pentagon's multiple independently targetable reentry vehicle). Can a piece you've written for one audience/type of publication work in another context?

  - For example, my *Food with Thought: The Wit and Wisdom of Chinese Fortune Cookies* was initially an idea for a page-a-day calendar. It could also be repurposed as an *Everything I Know I Learned from Fortune Cookie Fortunes* poster, or a collection of greeting cards.

  - *My Briefing for the Boardroom and the Situation Room* was initially lesson plans for a course I teach. I'll also use some of its tips in a later chapter.

  - My continuing series of terrorism chronologies started as data from my doctoral dissertation.

- ■ My seven volumes of terrorist biographies were sparked by an offhand remark from a fan.

- ☐ Consider **verges**—taking a thought from one environment and placing it in another environment.

- ☐ Stay **focused**. Keep your eye on the ball. Do things that get you to your goal. Always write or research **something each day**—keep the ball moving toward the goal line.

- ☐ **Don't do** things that keep you from getting to the goal line.

- ☐ Do a **crossword puzzle**—at least you wrote some words today, and the clues and answers might just spark a new idea!

- ☐ Get it down first. **Do not self-edit initially**.

- ☐ **Don't over-edit**. Get out of your own way.

- ☐ **Touch** a piece of paper **once**, decide what to do with it, do it, and move on.

- ☐ **Do the tedious, now**. Don't let it marinate in your in-box. It gets in the way of you getting anything else done.

- ☐ **Satisfice**. The perfect is the enemy of productivity. You can polish forever, until you wear the project down to nothing.

- ☐ When the **muse** hits, drop everything and start writing; don't lose the creativity spurt.

- ☐ Consider **collaborating**, particularly in areas in

which you're not adept. I'm collaborating on what is for me a new endeavor—novels. I've collaborated with an editor on indexing my terrorism books. I've also worked with dozens of friends in compiling two mini-memoirs collections, *Stories from Langley* and its sequel.

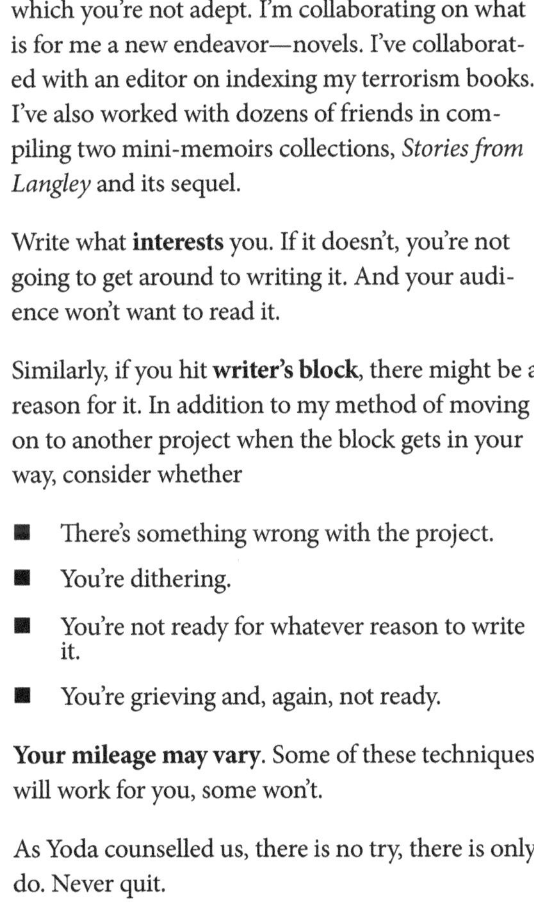

❑ Write what **interests** you. If it doesn't, you're not going to get around to writing it. And your audience won't want to read it.

❑ Similarly, if you hit **writer's block**, there might be a reason for it. In addition to my method of moving on to another project when the block gets in your way, consider whether

- There's something wrong with the project.
- You're dithering.
- You're not ready for whatever reason to write it.
- You're grieving and, again, not ready.

❑ **Your mileage may vary.** Some of these techniques will work for you, some won't.

❑ As Yoda counselled us, there is no try, there is only do. Never quit.

❑ Have **faith** in yourself. If I can do it, you can do it.

That's enough from me. Now go write something!

NOTES:

Be(coming) a Prolific Novelist

The steps it takes to write a novel are slightly different from those used in nonfiction. Here's what you are facing:

- ❑ Novel Overview/Elevator Speech

- ❑ Key Characters Bible: photos, motivations, goals, backstory

- ❑ Major Plot line of march

- ❑ Secondary plot(s) line of march

- ❑ First Chapter

- ❑ Final Chapter

- ❑ Outline how to get from A to Z

- ❑ Query letter

- ❑ Search (trademark and deep Google) the book's title to deconflict with other authors

- ❑ Send sample chapters, preferably A, B, C and Z, if requested

- ❑ Write chapters B through Y

- ❑ To Readers Group
- ❑ To Agent
- ❑ Incorporate Agent comments
- ❑ To Acquisitions Editor at publishing house
- ❑ Incorporate Acquisitions Editor Comments
- ❑ To Copy Editor (publishing house will do this)
- ❑ Answer Copy Editor questions
- ❑ Fill in Marketing Questionnaire
- ❑ Update Author Page on Amazon, B&N, Goodreads, others
- ❑ Get blurbs
- ❑ Create book-specific website
- ❑ Update personal author website
- ❑ Review Galleys
- ❑ Review Page Proofs
- ❑ Book release party at local bookstore
- ❑ Radio, Press, tv, blogs, other publicity
- ❑ Start writing sequel(s)

Collaboration with Another Author

Sometimes you have a great idea for a book, but you know that you're not the right writer to bring it to fruition, due to limitations of, say, your skill set or the amount of time you can devote to the project. But you don't want the world to lose your Great Idea. What to do?

It's time to consider **collaborating**, or co-authoring.

There are certain keys to successful collaboration:

First, figure out why you **need** to collaborate. What skills do you **lack** that you could find in someone else? If you're putting together an anthology, what experiences do others have that are more compelling/diverse/relevant than your own?

Second, find someone who **complements** your skill set. What is it that they bring to the table that adds to what you can do alone? Consider the Economics 101 principle of comparative advantage: What do you do best, and what do they do best—or at least better than you? Are there areas in which you two make up for each other's deficiencies? What do you do well, but for whatever reason, don't want to do (Self-editing, indexing and proofreading often come to mind for writers.)?

Third, make sure that you **respect** each other's contribution. While Mensans may be used to being called the "smartest person in the room", we haven't cornered the market on talent, insight, or drive. (In many cases, we're Mensans and they're not *only* because we decided to apply!) Whenever I'm considering collaborating, I read the other person's work in the medium in which I'm considering writing—novels, screenplays, nonfiction research on a topic new to me, knowledge of an arcane area, new developments in the business of publishing, and marketing. (Wow. I don't know a lot! Admitting what you don't know is crucial to successful partnering.) My co-author on *White Noise Whispers* has such a gift with language—bon mots, asides, les mots justes, descriptive flourishes, and the like—that I sometimes just sit back and savor what she's written for the sheer joy of watching a first-class mind in operation.

Fourth, be in constant **communication** with your partner. Bounce ideas off each other. Read each other's work and comment extensively on it. Don't just say "sounds good to me". You're trying to put together the best possible product your combined talents can create. My collaborations routinely generate hundreds of e-mails, phone calls, and meetings per project.

Fifth, be clear in what your **division of labor**/responsibilities will be. If you want a written contract, write one. If it's a handshake agreement, draft an informal list of who will do what. This list will differ depending upon the skills of your partner for each project. For *Take My Weight, Please*, I designed the organization of the book and wrote the text. My co-author, a fitness coach, developed the exercises and overall philosophy of the workout program. Another colleague photographed models using the gym equipment. For the *White Noise Whispers* murder mystery, I wrote the character bible (backstories, physical descriptions, and motivations of the 50 characters we used), the chapter-by-chapter plotline, and the concept of the book, then contacted psychiatrists, naturalists, and law enforcement professionals who offered insights into investigative tradecraft. Co-author Tracy Tripp developed the characters and plot, visited the likely body dump sites for verisimilitude, and wrote the finished product. Another novelist was happy just to let me develop the general concept of a retired serial killer at a 55+ community and do the proofreading. I'm now collaborating with a movie producer who lives in the world of screenplay writing, letting us take an idea for novel in a new (for me), and perhaps lucrative, direction.

Sixth, don't be embarrassed to offer an idea that eventually doesn't work. Your partner will see things from an entirely different **perspective**, and could build upon the idea, or take it in a direction that is ultimately far better than you would have by yourself. That's why you collaborated in the first place.

Here are a few of my collaborations. More to come.

NOTES:

Multi-Author Collaboration

Beyond these two-author collaboration tips, there are certain **keys to successful multi-author collaboration**:

If you're putting together an anthology, consider what experiences do others have that are more compelling/diverse/relevant than your own. Contact those writers.

Other things to **keep in mind** with mass collaborations:

You might think that having 20 authors is a **force multiplier**, yielding 20X increases in the likelihood of getting an agent, publicizing by social media, exploiting contacts in the industry, and getting regional reviews/newspaper-radio-tv-podcast interviews. It will not. Most authors will believe that they've taken care of their duties to the book project by submitting their chapter. Some authors will help you with the post-drafting aspects of book publishing. Most will move on to their next project.

Not everyone works to your **schedule**. Life happens among authors. Your expectations for prompt chapter deliveries and who will write what will quickly erode. Sometimes they just cannot complete the chapter on time (pro tip: be flexible), sometimes they are stuck on where the plot should go. When the latter happens, I let the author write another chapter downstream and call upon the next author in the queue.

Authors will also sometimes **not be available**, period. I've had authors die, ghost, take ill, get a great offer from a movie studio or Big Five publisher, or have to drop out for other reasons. Accept this gracefully. In some cases, the dropouts may be available for another project, or at least a blurb or review.

The **paperwork can be exhausting**. You're now communicating (via email, text, phone, smoke signals) with 20 other writers. This can be a huge time sink, siphoning time you could devote to other projects.

If you self-publish the book, you're on the hook for sending out 20 **royalty checks** each time payments are due. If you have a decent seller, you also have to generate 20 **1099s**, and let the IRS know via a 1096. And depending upon the state in which you and your author(s) reside, you might also need to inform the local and state taxation authorities.

If you go with a commercial house, you will want to hire a **contracts attorney** familiar with (or specializing in) the publishing business—a garden-variety attorney just won't do—to make sure that the contract presented sufficiently covers your and your colleagues' interests. It's very easy for a "civilian" author to make contract mistakes by saying "looks good to me". Are you signing away rights (electronic, movie, serialization, first refusal) that you want to retain? Does the publisher have an odd definition of "net proceeds" that is unfavorable to your bottom line? On a side note, the contributing authors might have idiosyncratic ideas about what the contract should include and how it should be phrased. Publishing houses usually prefer one-size-fits all language. Some of your authors will not.

Have the authors guaranteed that any **photos/graphics** are public domain or they have obtained permissions from the creators? Do the authors retain all rights to the texts (i.e., if they have been published before, they have **permission** to reprint)?

It's up to you to ensure **continuity** of the story and the characters. Height, weight, eye color, and other aspects of the characters must be consistent across chapters, or if they've changed, the reason is stated in the text. It's up to you to write the initial **character bible**, and add to it as chapters roll in. Compare the descriptions in the latest chapter to what the bible says. If necessary amend the chapter.

It's up to you to ensure that the story flows and makes sense. The threads must ultimately tie together and there cannot be any **unresolved** subplots (unless you state that a sequel is in the works).

You're working with at times fragile or strong **egos**. Making **developmental** editorial changes can be a give-and-take ordeal. **Typo, usage, and spelling corrections** usually are accepted without a fuss, although their number is often a surprise to even veteran authors.

Saying "no" to a contribution is never fun. While this is obviously part of the responsibilities of an organizer, it is difficult to reject a piece you had requested from a colleague. It may be that the colleague simply does not understand the purpose of the contribution, or the book has gone in a different direction, or the piece just is not up to your standards. Whatever the reason for rejection, it requires a compassionate touch. It is doubtful that you will be in the position to request a piece again directly from the author, although it's possible that they will respond to an indirect general call for submissions.

Despite what seems to be a litany of negatives, I've greatly enjoyed collaborating on two- and multiple-author projects. It's also fascinating to see another creative mind expanding your initial idea, making for a better product.

And you'll find that you deepen friendships along the way.

Here are a few of my collaborations. More to come.

**Remember, buy my books,
or the forces of evil win.**

Character Bibles

Among the more embarrassing things that can happen to a fiction writer are unintended changes in a character. These can include

- physical discrepancies (the protagonist has blue eyes on page 4, and brown eyes on page 115; she's petite and not athletic on page 6, but jumps center—without an impressive vertical leap—on page 324)

- resume shifts (protagonist was a University of Michigan biology major on page 5, but a statistics major at Tufts on page 39)

- changes in relationship status (married on page 6, unmarried without explanation (divorce, widowed, abandonment) on page 56)

- spelling of the protagonist's name (Jim on page 3, Jimi on page 36, back to Jim on page 79, without explanation for the changes in the identifier)

Keeping all of the little details about 50 or 60 characters in your head while you're writing a fast-paced thriller with descriptive details about settings, organizations, and key twists in the plot can be daunting, even for those of us with photographic memories. It's easy to forget what you wrote about an ancillary character 18 days ago. Movie producers hire continuity professionals to make sure these errors don't occur across scenes. These specialists frequently photograph the scene when the director yells "cut" just so when the editors begin organizing the flow of the story, characters are standing precisely where they were a few seconds ago, wearing the same clothing, with the same cloud patterns and airplanes moving behind them, and the like. They're well aware of the legions of nitpickers who create online groups to carp about continuity errors and anachronisms.

You can ensure against continuity errors in your fiction by creating **character bibles**—detailed descriptions, including back stories, of every character who appears in the story. You need not use every detail you're written in these descriptions—show, don't tell—but they'll help guide you in thinking about what makes each character tick. A typical bible entry might include

- role of the character—main character/protagonist, antagonist, love interest, sidekick, staff, incidental walk-on, cameo from another volume in the novel series

- physical descriptions—height, weight, posture, eye color, age, gender, hair color

- activities—hobbies, food preferences, sports, pets, smoking/vaping, drug use, drinking habits

- relationships and connections, including familial, dating, professional

- work and school affiliations

- motivation(s)

- what is to be revealed about the character as the story develops, what some characters will not initially—or never—know about the character

There's no rule about what to include or not include—write a bible that helps you.

Consider putting photos of the characters on a whiteboard just behind your computer screen. You can get photos from thispersondoesnotexist.com (which ensures that you're not writing for a specific Hollywood actor) or by running a search in an images catalog for, say, "20-year-old blond woman" or "45-year-old Eurasian man with a face tattoo".

Here's an example of what Tracy Tripp, my *White Noise Whispers* coauthor, and I used for our main character:

The Detective: Jim Castile

- Former Army MP in Iraq

- Junior detective, often passed over for promotion, resentful

- Open to raising a family

- Tinkers with his 1971 M151 A2 Jeep

- Knee injury in football

Note how using a photo saves us from having to write down every physical detail of the character. A quick glance reminds us of, e.g., hair color, race, beard length, apparent age.

Some writers find it helpful to share the bibles with the reader. In the theater, a very short version of a bible is the dramatis personae listing in the *Playbill*. Mario Puzo often introduced characters with two-page back stories before bringing his characters into an ongoing scene. Use as much or as little as you need to maintain the narrative velocity of the storytelling.

Buy my books, or the people
who say "somewhat unique" win.

Commercial Publishing

At some point, usually while you're still writing, sometimes when you have a first draft, you'll be faced with the post-writing issue: Where/how am I going to get this thing published?

You have two basic options—going to an established publishing house, and self-publishing. I've done both, having used seven traditional commercial firms and trying the DIY route. The pluses and minuses listed below apply to any format—books, blogs, articles, postings; I'll use "book" as a shorthand.

In this chapter we'll focus on traditional, or commercial, publishing.

Advantages of Commercial Publishing

- They handle advertising and distribution.

- They have numerous catalogs that go to specialized clients.

- They'll send review copies to whatever publications you designate, at no cost to you.

- They handle the accounting, particularly welcome if you have to keep tabs on sales tax.

- An army of editors, copyeditors, proofreaders, layout editors, graphic designers, and indexers will make your manuscript a better book.

Drawbacks of Commercial Publishing

- Acquisitions editors have large "slush piles" (unsolicited over-the-transom submissions) and can take forever (they usually counsel three months) to get back to you, if they ever do.

- Some acquisitions editors frown on simultaneous submissions. Ignore them. If they answer at all, and it's a "no", you've lost three months.

- Can take what seems like forever to get it on the streets. My nonfiction usually takes a year from the time the manuscript is accepted.

- The bureaucracy of the house's publishing process can be overwhelming. They will often ask for a one-page summary, a three-page summary, a first chapter, an outline, text for the back cover, text for the press kit, text for the media announcement, and detailed answers to a long Author Questionnaire.

- The editors will want you to make changes that you might not welcome.

- The large houses, and even the smaller ones, often require an agent (virtually mandatory for fiction, especially for lesser-known authors, and increasingly needed for nonfiction). However, an agent's fee—usually 10-15%—can be worth it. The right agent opens doors to publishers, helps you create a better manuscript, knows the pitfalls of publishing contracts, and can negotiate a better deal. Find one specializing in your genre. Some are particularly adept at movie deals, audiobooks, and the like.

■ The often-overriding concern of commercial houses is not the quality of the manuscript but its projected sales figures.

■ Ad budgets for new authors are minimal. You will not be jetting to a 40-city tour, staying in five-star hotels. Houses expect your query letter to include how your previous books have sold, the extent of your audience contacts (often measured by website hits and Facebook author page likes), and what you will do to promote the book. (They'll ask you this again in their Author Questionnaire if they express interest.)

■ Sometime they'll ask you for suggested blurbers; sometimes you have to contact the blurb writers.

Whew! That doesn't sound like fun. Maybe self-publishing is better. We'll discuss that option next month.

**Buy my books, or the people who mistake
you're, your, yore, and all y'all's win.**

NOTES:

DIY Publishing

In the previous chapter, we explored the ins and outs of publishing with a traditional commercial publisher. Let's now look at the growing field of do-it-yourself or self-publishing.

Advantages of DIY Publishing

- Very fast turnaround, particularly attractive if you're writing on current events, a major scientific/intellectual breakthrough, or controversial topics with short legs.

- You get to say exactly what you want.

- You get a much larger royalty percentage of the purchase price.

Drawbacks of DIY Publishing

- You're tempted to release a book before it's ready. I'm not suggesting you follow an ancient philosopher's advice to let it marinate for 10 years, but let it sit for a while, then come back to it with fresh eyes.

- You have to take care of all of the back-end of publishing. Not only do you get the fun part—

researching and writing—but you also have to obtain the ISBNs for each type of publication (e.g., hardcover, e-book), register the copyright, contact individual bookstores to get your book on the shelves (many stores don't welcome DIY projects and send you to Ingram-Spark), pay for ads, find reviewers, pay for the review copies, pay for shipping for the review copies, curate the book's dedicated website, curate your website, schedule and conduct radio/television/podcast interviews, obtain newspaper and magazine interviews, address book clubs, civic associations, and anyone else looking for a speaker (I can coach you on public speaking if you need it), inter alia. You may find that this administrivia takes more time than producing the manuscript did.

■ "Self-publishing" is often viewed as being a cut below "real" publishing with a brick and mortar house. Some observers say you're not a "real" author until someone else has said "I want to buy your manuscript because I think we can make money from it." Others point to the lack of editorial vetting, and the dismal sales record of the preponderance of self-published books. A 90% royalty on 0 sales is still 0.

Ultimately, the decision comes down to you. Which are you comfortable with? How much time and money are you willing to invest in your project? Sometimes the decision is made for you—you have not been able to attract an agent or acquisitions editor.

The bottom line: consider the bottom line for your writing. What motivates you? Are you writing for the money? For the sense of satisfaction? For the opportunity to add to the world's knowledge? The answers to these questions can also help you decide which of these two routes to take. Good luck. And keep writing.

Buy my books, or the
(insert your joke here;
send them to me on edmickolus@hotmail.com,
and we'll use the funniest in upcoming columns)
win.

NOTES:

Financial Issues

In the last few chapters, we've talked about some of the pluses and minuses of the traditional publishing vs. do-it-yourself (DIY) routes. Now let's consider their financial aspects.

Publishing finance revolves around the question of risk. In the olden days, when dinosaurs and traditional publishing ruled, your book got published when an editorial board at a publishing house determined "we can make money off the sales of this author's book. We don't know how many books it will sell, but it shows promise." Until then, you were a writer, not an author. The house was willing to assume all of the risk of publishing, i.e., the possibility of them not recouping their investment in producing, marketing, and distributing the book.

Thus, the standard model for publishing with a conventional publisher became: They pay all production fees, and may even give you an advance. After recouping costs, they would give the author a royalty, usually around 10-15% of the net price of the book. Sometimes you might get a progressive rate, based upon specified sales targets. If you made the sales targets, your royalty % ratcheted up. If you sold millions—say, if you're John Grisham—your rate would be even higher, sometimes with a set higher rate independent of absolute sales figures.

The houses argue that this arrangement is fair, as they have assumed the risk up front. If your book doesn't sell, they have to eat those costs.

Nontraditional houses, including subsidy publishers, DIY, and other arrangements, have flipped the template for publishing risk, passing it from the house to the author.

Subsidy publishers charge you up front for all of their production, marketing, and distribution costs, then pay you back until you've recouped your costs, after which they pay you a royalty, generally substantially above what you'd get with a conventional publisher. These can run to 70% or so. They've shifted the risk onto you. If the book doesn't sell, they still make money. If the book sells, they also make money.

Selectively financed self-publishing can eliminate the middle man. You pay for services that you need up front, then get the proceeds from sales. You pay only for what you need.

Some subsidy publishers try to get you to pay for things you don't need, including

- their editorial services, even though you've used another service

- cover design, even though you've used your own graphics shop

- proofreading

and the like. Avoid them.

Separate from the above two models, and of far less regard in the publishing industry, are the vanity houses, which charge you for all of the services, print a given number of books, and ship them to you, where they'll molder in your garage. Avoid them, too, unless your book is designed to be a gift for family members only.

No matter how many titles you have published, always do a web search of other authors' experience with a publisher you are considering. The results can be eye-opening, and save you lots of investment, both emotional and financial.

Remember: Buy my books,
or the Forces of Evil win.

NOTES:

Managing Marketing Departments: Dusting Your Dust Jacket

You've dutifully followed my suggestions and put together your first book. You've polished it through a dozen drafts, shared it with colleagues and experts, researched the market, obtained representation, shepherded it through the commercial publishing acquisitions and editing process, proofed three iterations of galleys and page proofs, obtained blurbs, ordered the wine and cheese for your release party, and are ready to unleash your Great American Novel/ Non-Fiction Insights on an unsuspecting audience.

Here's where the Marketing Department comes in.

At some point, you'll receive a long Author Questionnaire. In addition to straightforward stuff ("What's your Social Security number? To what address do we send your royalty check?"), you'll be asked for names/addresses of likely newspapers/journals/other outlets likely to review your book; worthies who would be willing to blurb your book; and details of your "platform" (those who follow you on social media, in professional journals and conferences, etc.). While it's a chore to fill out, it's critical that you provide them with as much detail as possible.

Shrinking marketing budgets mean that the days of your jetting off to scores of cities on a whirlwind signing tour are over. Most houses can afford to spring for review copies and little else, and do not have robust teams able to research other outlets for your book. They generally look to you for leadership in flogging your book. (You should detail your platform and ability to market your book as the third paragraph of your query letter introducing yourself to the house's relevant acquisitions editor.)

Marketing departments differ widely in what other services they will provide. You can generally count on getting mentioned in their catalogues, which come out with various frequencies. Some catalogues are tailored to specific markets, others merely to anyone who might pick up a book that year (book readership demographics are dismal.).

In rare instances, you'll run across a house that has great hopes for your book, and will go the extra mile. I was blessed by having Pelican Publishers pick up my *Secret Book of CIA Humor* as one of their projects. Thanks to their toils, I was interviewed by Scott Simon for a Saturday morning *NPR* broadcast, *BBC World* (and its 40 million listeners worldwide), *America in the Morning*, and numerous regional radio stations. A host of signing events led to an interview with the *Sunday Times of London*. It was a heady experience to walk out of the Washington, D.C. *NPR* headquarters and be asked by tourists if I was someone famous. (I was for those 10 seconds! I'm now back to being a denizen of the mid-lists…)

Attentiveness to details on the dust jacket is crucial if you send review copies to journals and newspapers whose reviewers are pressed for time to read your book, and simply quote from the dust jacket notes (as has happened to me several times; but then, it's nice to see your words in print, twice!).

Although Marketing folk have more experience than you in flogging books, they don't know your topic as well as you do, and can make factual/terminology errors. For example, a friend's recent spy-fi best seller's dust jacket had these groaners:

- "CIA agents" Folks in the U.S. Government who carry a gun and a badge call themselves agents (FBIrs like to be called Special Agents.). Everyone who works in the CIA are *intelligence officers*. Directorate of Operations recruiters are "operations officers", or sometimes "core collectors", but not "agents", which is the less-common term for "assets" or "sources", i.e., foreigners stealing secrets for us.

- "Russia *Division*", where most of the novel takes place, doesn't exist. It's now called Central Eurasian Division (CE is the common term; one rarely hears "Central Eurasian Division" voiced.). A more common reference is Russia House, which is a subunit of CE within the Directorate of Operations.

- "Departments" exist as various Cabinet organizations, but even when CIA is a Cabinet member (probably just a fond memory now that we have a Director of National Intelligence), CIA isn't called a Department. There is a "department" subunit in one DO center; the term isn't used anywhere else.

- CIA does not have "Field Stations". Non-Headquarters FBI facilities are "field offices", although more currently they're using "division" for some, but not all, facilities to further muddy the waters. CIA's Moscow facility would be "Moscow Station". A subservient affiliate of the Station, usually found in a national capital city, is a Base, usually found outside the capital city.

If I didn't know the author and her work, I may well have put the book back on the shelf. (As it turns out, she didn't write the dust jacket notes.)

While these details might not matter to the typical reader, these gaffes can quickly erode the credibility of an author in the eyes of professionals in the given field of the novel. When I was writing *Spycraft for Thriller Writers*, the "CIA agents" error was most often cited by Agency colleagues as their chief irritant with spy movies, tv shows, and novels.

Bottom line: If you can, write your own dust jacket notes. Failing that, make sure the Marketing Department scribe gets 'em right! It's another tedious task en route to publication, but worth it in the end.

Public Speaking for Authors

Although you view yourself as a writer, maybe not as a speaker, you'll often be called upon to address groups regarding your book, or the topic of your book, or writing in general. There are numerous issues you can handle beforehand that can increase the likelihood of your giving an effective public address. You should consider:

- Jitters

- Speaking Styles and Delivery

- Getting Organized

- Know your Environment

- Know your Audience (in the room)

- Let's Get Graphic

- Answering Questions

- Follow Up

What the above constitutes is a "**roadmap**" for this chapter. Roadmaps are an excellent practice for giving a speech. Tell the audience up front what issues you're going to cover. It will give them an idea as to whether they're in the correct room, and what you might not cover but can be coaxed into addressing during the Q&A session. Always have a Q&A session—it keeps the audience engaged and in their seats.

The first thing to consider is stage fright, often called **jitters**. We have a fear of failure, particularly failing in a public setting. How to combat this?

One way is to consider what can possibly go wrong that would lead to embarrassment. Then figure out how you can prevent this situation from happening. For example:

- A colleague was briefing a senior official one-on-one in the interlocutor's office. The briefer tended to have wide gestures, and accidentally knocked the principal's coffee into his lap. The simple fix: move your chair sufficiently far from the principal's desk so that your wingspan is no longer a worry.

- You forget your next point. Simple fix: write your points on index cards. The principal will appreciate your wanting to get things right, rather than memorized. The great tv talk show hosts and *Saturday Night Live* cast members put their monologues and lines on cue cards. If it's ok for them, it's ok for you.

- A colleague dropped her note cards. Simple fix: number each of them.

There are a host of other pitfalls, and solutions, which I cover in my *Briefing for the Boardroom and the Situation Room.*

Another technique is to keep in mind that the audience wants you to succeed. They decided to come to your presentation, rather than do lots of other things that begged for their attention. Moreover, they've made public speaking unforced errors in their careers, and will understand if/when you do.

Sometimes the host will cut your time due to unplanned exigencies. Make sure that you have a shorter version of your presentation, and that you cover your main points up front.

We all have our own **speaking styles**, some of which help us—great pronunciation, energy, enthusiasm, confidence, eye contact—some of which don't—uptalk, vocal fry, verbal graffiti/filler words (um, er, uh, ya know), Valley-speak (I'm like vice I said), speaking too quickly or too slowly for the room, jargon, acronym-rich environment, slanguage. Simple fix: Pause. While it feels to you like an interminable amount of time, it's saying to the audience "I want to give you time to absorb that last point." And as for the other oddities, simply make your delivery conversational. Don't talk down to the audience, talk with them.

In **organizing** your presentation, make the key point of your speech the organizing principle. Are you trying to introduce yourself to an audience? Get them to buy your book? Develop your talk around that. Start with your bottom line up front. It may be that your presentation will be cut short— at least they'll leave the room with your key point firmly established. Then give them the roadmap—here's what we'll cover. It can't hurt to practice out loud—you'll spot tongue twisters you would miss by simple silent reading.

You should have a firm grasp of your **environment**— sight lines (can they see your slides), sound (if there's a microphone available, use it), security (are you going to have demonstrators outside in the parking lot, or closer), do you need to bring credentials to get in the door, what's the dress code, is your computer compatible with the facility's A/V system?

You should also know the **audience**, especially who is the audience's leader. What's the size of the audience? Audience dynamics with five people are different from a group of 5,000. How do they address one another? Is there any in-group patois you should know? Is it ok to shake hands? What do they want to know (sometimes called the WIIFM—What's In It For Me?) and what do they already know?

Graphics can aid your presentation when used correctly and sabotage it if used ineptly. Have you experienced Death by Powerpoint, in which the speaker has too many words on the slide, and reads every one of them? There is a difference between handouts (which can have as many words as you want), slides (the fewer words and the more compelling the graphic, the better), and your talking points (which are *not* your slides nor your handouts and should be seen only by you via your index cards).

Consider when you want to give the audience your handouts. Do you want them to read ahead, read along, or read after the presentation? Choose images that bolster your words, not distract from them. While there are also sorts of cool things you can do with graphics, it does not mean that you must. Get the message across, rather than have them say "I wonder how s/he got that cool animation effect on that slide?". There is no magic number for the amount of slides to use, nor a magic number for amount of words for each slide. The more concise, the better.

A very effective graphic can be your book cover. It puts your cover again in the mind of the audience. You can also use maps, photos, charts, and other tools, so long as there is no clutter on the slide. Fonts can help or hurt. Use fonts that are easy to read rather than **cool for the sake of being cool** and are really hard to read. Color can be your friend, but be kind to the color-blind and keep in mind that you want contrast in your choice of backgrounds and foregrounds.

Questions are a priori scary (what if I can't answer something?) but can be an opportunity. A few tips:

- If an audience member wants to ask a question during your presentation, give a short answer and say "we'll explore this in more depth later." Do not say "please hold your questions till the end." The audience member will turn you off, thinking about what their unanswered question is and thinking that you've been rude.

- If you temporarily blank, you can gain a few seconds by saying "That's a question we've been wrestling with." This should give you enough time to come up for air. Do not say, however, "That's a great question." Everyone else in the audience who has asked a question will be thinking "so you didn't like my question?".

- If you really do not know the answer say, "I don't know at the moment but I'll research the issue and get back to you." Do so. "I don't know" means "everything else I've told you I've said with confidence and I wasn't trying to snow you with bafflegab. You can trust what I've said."

- Make sure to check the news that morning. Sometimes a development will affect the subject of your presentation.

Just because the oral part of your speech is over doesn't mean the presentation is over. Make sure to **follow up** on the questions you promised to answer, collect business cards to set up your next talks, thank the host, and sell a few books along the way!

NOTES:

Books by Edward Mickolus

TERRORISM

Terrorist Events Worldwide, 2025

Terrorist Events Worldwide, 2023-2024

Terrorist Events Worldwide, 2022

Terrorist Events Worldwide, 2021

Terrorist Events Worldwide 2019-2020

Terrorism Worldwide, 2018

Terrorism Worldwide, 2017

Terrorism Worldwide, 2016

Terrorism 2013-2015: A Worldwide Chronology

Terrorism 2008-2012: A Worldwide Chronology

Terrorism, 2005-2007

with Susan L. Simmons *Terrorism, 2002-2004: A Chronology 3 volumes*

with Susan L. Simmons *Terrorism, 1996-2001: A Chronology of Events and a Selectively Annotated Bibliography 2 volumes*

with Susan L. Simmons *Terrorism, 1992-1995: A Chronology of Events and a Selectively Annotated Bibliography*

Terrorism, 1988-1991: A Chronology of Events and a Selectively Annotated Bibliography

with Todd Sandler and Jean Murdock *International Terrorism in the 1980s: A Chronology, Volume 2: 1984-1987*

with Todd Sandler and Jean Murdock *International Terrorism in the 1980s: A Chronology, Volume 1: 1980-1983*

Transnational Terrorism: A Chronology of Events, 1968 1979

with Peter Flemming *Terrorism, 1980-1987: A Selectively Annotated Bibliography*

The Literature of Terrorism: A Selectively Annotated Bibliography

Annotated Bibliography on International and Transnational Terrorism available in *Legal and Other Aspects of Terrorism*

International Terrorism: Attributes of Terrorist Events, 1968-1977, ITERATE 2 Data Codebook

ITERATE: International Terrorism: Attributes of Terrorist Events, Data Codebook

Combatting International Terrorism: A Quantitative Analysis

with Susan L. Simmons *The 50 Worst Terrorist Attacks*

with Susan L. Simmons *The Terrorist List: North America*

with Susan L. Simmons *The Terrorist List: South America*

with Susan L. Simmons *The Terrorist List: Eastern Europe*

with Susan L. Simmons *The Terrorist List: Western Europe*

with Susan L. Simmons *The Terrorist List: Asia, Pacific, and Sub-Saharan Africa*

The Terrorist List: The Middle East, 2 volumes

INTELLIGENCE

Spycraft for Thriller Writers: How to Write Spy Novels and Movies Accurately and Not Be Laughed at by Real-Life Spies

More Stories from Langley: Another Glimpse Inside the CIA

Stories from Langley: A Glimpse Inside the CIA

The Counterintelligence Chronology: Spying by and Against the United States from the 1700s through 2014

The Secret Book of Intelligence Community Humor

Two Spies Walk Into a Bar

The Secret Book of CIA Humor

INSPIRATION

Harlan Rector and Ed Mickolus, eds. I Still Matter: Finding Meaning in Life at All Ages

Harlan Rector and Ed Mickolus, eds. I Matter Too: Finding Meaning in Life at All Ages

Harlan Rector and Ed Mickolus, eds. I Matter: Finding Meaning in Life at All Ages

His Words: Inspirational Quotations from Jesus Christ

EDUCATION

Beyond Authorship: Things Writers Should Know Besides How to Write

The Creativity Sourcebook

Briefing for the Boardroom and the Situation Room

with Joseph T. Brannan *Coaching Winning Model United Nations Teams*

HUMOR

More Funny COVID Memes

America's Funniest Memes: Coronavirus Edition

Food with Thought: The Wit and Wisdom of Chinese Fortune Cookies

MISCELLANY

Famous Last Meals

All the Presidents' Heroes: Inspirational Stories of the Honorees of the State of the Union Addresses, 7 volumes

> *Volume 1: Ronald Reagan*
>
> *Volume 2: George H. W. Bush*
>
> *Volume 3: William Jefferson Clinton*
>
> *Volume 4: George W. Bush*
>
> *Volume 5: Barack Obama*
>
> *Volume 6: Donald J. Trump*
>
> *Volume 7: Joseph R. Biden*

with Bill Wildey *Trivia Matters: A Trivia Host Sourcebook*

with Joe Rendon *Take My Weight, Please; Head-to-Toe Fitness for Seniors—The Cowboy Joe Way*

FICTION

with Carmen Amato, Gina Bennett, Tony Cipparone, Clint Collins, Jeff Grant, Mark Henshaw, Ralph Hughes, Laura Manning Johnson, Blaine McCants, Susan Ouellette, Anthony Patton, Julie Savell-McCandless, Janice Sebring, Paula T. Weiss *Moscow Syndrome*

with Scott M. Baker, Clint Collins, Gene Coyle, Anne Gruner, Jay Gruner, James Lawler, Clint Mesle, Susan Ouellette, Valerie Plame, Bill Rapp, Julie Savell-McCandless, Janice Sebring, J.R. Seeger, Paula T. Weiss, Terry Williams *Naked Came the Spy*

with Tracy Tripp *…and Presumed Dead (working title)*

with Tracy Tripp *White Noise Whispers*

Stories by the Side of the Road

About Edward Mickolus

Ed Mickolus graduated from Georgetown University and obtained MA, MPhil, and PhD degrees from Yale University before anyone noticed they were missing. He worked as a staffer at the Central Intelligence Agency for 33 years and as an intelligence contractor for another seven years.

He served as CIA's first full-time analyst on international terrorism; analyzed African political, economic, social, military, and leadership issues; wrote political-psychological assessments of world leaders; managed collection, counter-intelligence, and covert action programs; and edited *What's News at CIA*.

He is the President of Vinyard Software, Inc. (www.vinyardsoftware.com), which produces terrorism events and biographic databases; clients include some 200 universities in 24 countries.

Its publishing arm is Wandering Woods Publishers. He teaches at various universities on writing, creativity, and intelligence.

His 60+ books cover such topics as international terrorism, international organization, education, intelligence, history, humor, inspiration, fitness, public speaking, and biography.

In addition to the above topics, his 100+ scholarly journal articles and book chapters also cover psychology, law, computers, the Internet, sociology, African politics, folklore, and automobile collection.

He has been interviewed on podcasts, by Faculti.net, NPR, BBC World, America in the Morning, and the Florida Times-Union, inter alia.

He is married to Susan Schjelderup; their daughter is Dr. Ciana Mickolus.

Please visit www.edwardmickolus.com

EdwardMickolus.com
VinyardSoftware.com

www.ingramcontent.com/pod-product-compliance
Lightning Source LLC
Chambersburg PA
CBHW050013040726
47599CB00014B/1365